TEXAS

ALASKA

CANADA

PACIFIC
OCEAN

UNITED
STATES

HAWAII

PUERTO
RICO

MEXICO

TEXAS

HELLO
U.S.A.

by Kathy Pelta

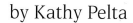
Lerner Publications Company

You'll find this picture of bluebonnet flowers at the beginning of each chapter. Named for its color and its resemblance to a woman's hat, the bluebonnet was chosen as Texas's state flower in 1901. Bluebonnet plants grow as tall as three feet. After rain, a drop of water can be found in each of the flower's blossoms.

Cover (left): An oil field at dusk. Cover (right): The Alamo in San Antonio. Pages 2–3: A cattle drive near downtown Dallas. Page 3: The reddish walls of mountains in Palo Duro Canyon State Park.

This book is available in two editions:
Library binding by Lerner Publications Company, a division of Lerner Publishing Group
Soft cover by First Avenue Editions, an imprint of Lerner Publishing Group
241 First Avenue North
Minneapolis, MN 55401 U.S.A.

Website address: www.lernerbooks.com

Library of Congress Cataloging-in-Publication Data

Pelta, Kathy.
    Texas / by Kathy Pelta. (Rev. and expanded 2nd ed.)
      p.   cm. — (Hello U.S.A.)
    Includes index.
    Summary: Introduces the geography, history, environment, economy, famous people, and culture of the Lone Star State.
    ISBN: 0–8225–4064–9 (lib. bdg. : alk. paper)
    ISBN: 0–8225–4142–4 (pbk. : alk. paper)
    1. Texas—Juvenile literature. [1. Texas.] I. Title. II. Series.
    F386.3 .P45 2002
    976.4—dc21   2001002958

Manufactured in the United States of America
1 2 3 4 5 6 – JR – 07 06 05 04 03 02

CONTENTS

A lone agave plant sits on the southern rim of the Chisos Mountains in Big Bend National Park.

THE LAND

Wild Frontier

T he thundering hooves of stampeding cattle. The noisy clunk of oil-drilling equipment. A flowering cactus in a deserted landscape. These are the sights and sounds that many people link to Texas. But this big, broad state—the second largest in the United States—also has mountains, grasslands, rivers, and miles of coastline.

Texas is a southern state, located midway between the Atlantic Ocean and the Pacific Ocean. Water shapes many of the state's borders.

Cowboys are not a thing of the past in Texas.

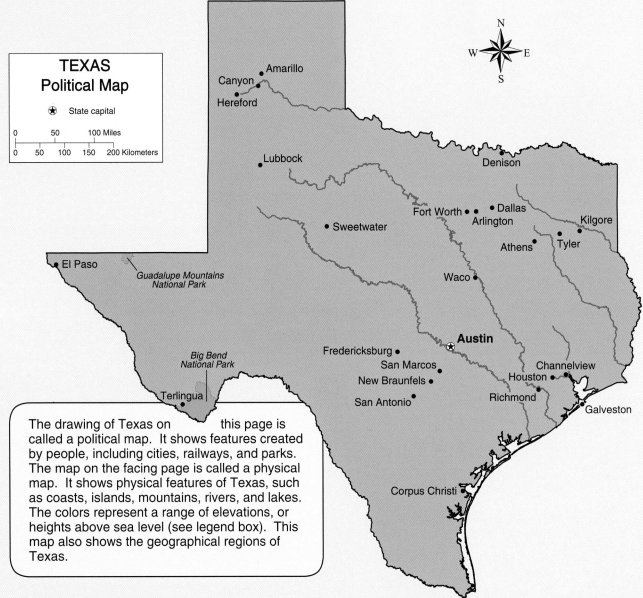

TEXAS
Political Map

⊛ State capital

```
0        50       100 Miles
0   50  100  150  200 Kilometers
```

N
W · E
S

Amarillo
Canyon
Hereford

Lubbock

Denison

Fort Worth · Dallas
Arlington

Kilgore

Sweetwater

Athens · Tyler

El Paso

Guadalupe Mountains National Park

Waco

Big Bend National Park

Austin

Fredericksburg
San Marcos
New Braunfels
San Antonio

Channelview
Houston
Richmond

Galveston

Terlingua

Corpus Christi

The drawing of Texas on   this page is called a political map. It shows features created by people, including cities, railways, and parks. The map on the facing page is called a physical map. It shows physical features of Texas, such as coasts, islands, mountains, rivers, and lakes. The colors represent a range of elevations, or heights above sea level (see legend box). This map also shows the geographical regions of Texas.

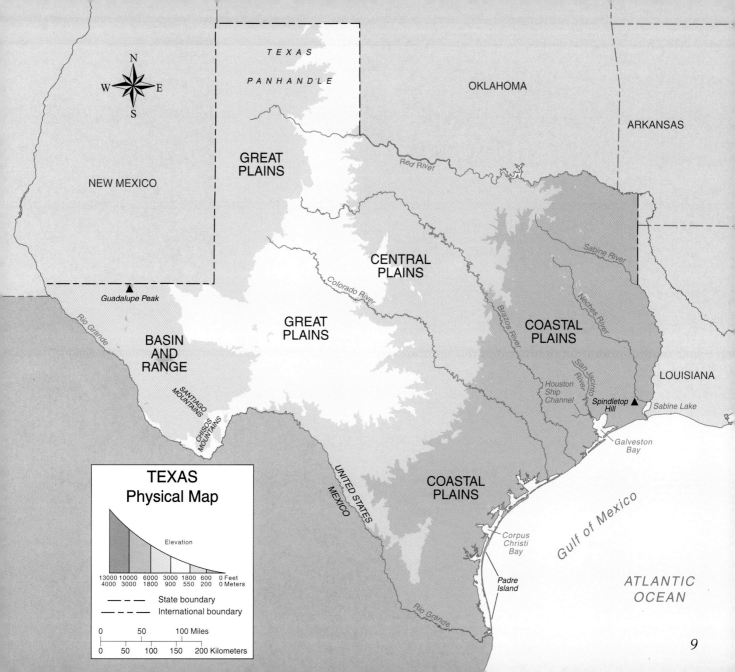

N
W · E
S

TEXAS PANHANDLE

OKLAHOMA

ARKANSAS

NEW MEXICO

GREAT PLAINS

Red River

Guadalupe Peak ▲

Rio Grande

BASIN AND RANGE

SANTIAGO MOUNTAINS

CHISOS MOUNTAINS

GREAT PLAINS

Colorado River

CENTRAL PLAINS

Sabine River

Brazos River

Neches River

COASTAL PLAINS

San Jacinto River

Houston Ship Channel

LOUISIANA

Spindletop Hill ▲

Sabine Lake

Galveston Bay

UNITED STATES
MEXICO

COASTAL PLAINS

Corpus Christi Bay

Padre Island

Rio Grande

Gulf of Mexico

ATLANTIC OCEAN

TEXAS
Physical Map

Elevation

13000	10000	6000	3000	1800	600	0 Feet
4000	3000	1800	900	550	200	0 Meters

— · — State boundary

— — — International boundary

0	50	100 Miles
0	50	100	150	200 Kilometers

9

A kayaker uses his paddle for balance as he navigates the muddy, turbulent waters of the Rio Grande.

Across the Red River, Texas's northern neighbors are Oklahoma and Arkansas. To the east, across the Sabine River, is Louisiana. New Mexico lies to the west. To the southwest, beyond the Rio Grande, is the country of Mexico.

The Gulf of Mexico—part of the Atlantic Ocean—marks the southeastern boundary of Texas. Narrow sandbars (islands of sand) lie offshore and protect Texas's Gulf coast from storms and strong winds. Bays, including Galveston Bay and Corpus Christi Bay, sit between the sandbars and the coast.

Most of Texas's rivers empty into the Gulf of Mexico. The state's longest waterways are the Rio Grande and the Red, Brazos, and Colorado Rivers.

Dams built across some rivers—such as the Neches and the Sabine—have created reservoirs, or artificial lakes. These lakes store freshwater for towns and cities throughout the state.

Four main land regions stretch across Texas. The land rises in height from the Gulf of Mexico in the southeast to Texas's western border. The regions are the Coastal Plains, the Central Plains, the Great Plains, and the Basin and Range region.

The low Coastal Plains spread north and west from the Gulf and cover one-third of the state. Warm weather helps farmers in the southern Coastal Plains grow many kinds of fruits and vegetables year-round. To the north, along the Louisiana border, fields of cotton, sugarcane, and rice thrive in the rich soil.

The warm climate of the southern Coastal Plains is ideal for growing cabbages.

West of the Coastal Plains lie the slightly higher Central Plains. Oil wells, farms, forests, and large cattle ranches share this rolling and rugged land with coyotes, foxes, and jackrabbits. In the 1800s, thousands of buffalo roamed here. Long before that, many dinosaurs did, too!

Even higher than the Central Plains are the Great Plains, which extend across most of western

The pump of this Central Plains oil well is decorated with a bucking bronco.

12

Texas. These plains are part of a vast region that stretches north all the way to Canada. Farmers on the Great Plains of Texas grow wheat and cotton. Huge herds of cattle, goats, and sheep feed on the region's hearty grasses.

The Great Plains include the nearly treeless Texas Panhandle. The area is named for its shape. The Panhandle juts northward from the rest of Texas and, on a map, looks a little like the handle on a saucepan.

The only mountains in Texas rise in the Basin and Range region of the southwest. Within this area, Guadalupe Peak, the highest point in the state, reaches 8,751 feet. In between the mountains are valleys that get little rainfall.

Huge sandstone rocks overlook the Texas Panhandle.

Within the mountain wilderness of the Basin and Range region, porcupines, mule deer, bears, and surefooted bighorn sheep wander. In dry areas, rattlesnakes and horned lizards look for shade beneath ocotillo shrubs and prickly pear cacti.

It's probably no surprise that in a state as large as Texas, the climate varies a lot from place to place. Warm, humid weather is typical on the Gulf coast. Hot, dry weather conditions are common in the southwest, while harsh winters chill the Texas Panhandle.

In Big Bend National Park, a bighorn sheep *(right)* basks in the sun. Ocotillo plants *(above)* also grow in abundance throughout the park.

The Basin and Range region, the state's hottest area, averages 60° F in January and 85° F in July. In the Panhandle, where temperatures are cooler, January's average temperature is 35° F, and July's is 79° F.

Texas is hit by more tornadoes than any other state. Each spring and summer, around 100 of these destructive, funnel-shaped clouds touch down, mainly in northern Texas. Hurricanes often blow in from the Gulf and strike the southern coast and the nearby sandbars.

Although Texas doesn't get much **precipitation,** most of it comes in the form of rain. The state's average rainfall every year is 27 inches. Most of the rain falls in the Coastal Plains. Hills in this region block rain clouds from moving farther inland. For this reason, much of the rest of Texas is dry. In some years, parts of southwestern Texas get less than 12 inches of rain.

Early people living in western Texas sometimes painted pictures on cave walls. These images were found in the Panther Cave, which is named for a panther painting that is more than 15 feet long.

THE HISTORY

The Lone Star State

The first people to live in what would become Texas probably came from the north more than 10,000 years ago. They were part of a large movement of people who crossed a land bridge from Asia to North America and then headed southward.

In Texas these early hunters and gatherers moved from place to place in search of wild plants and animals. The people hunted and butchered mammoths (hairy elephants) and giant bison for food. On the walls of their caves, early residents of Texas painted scenes of people, animals, and important religious events.

Karankawa Indians ate the oysters they found in the Gulf of Mexico *(left)*. The Karankawa ate lizards *(right)* when fishing was bad.

Later groups gathered seeds from wild plants and began to grow cotton, corn, beans, and squash. As food supplies became more dependable, the people no longer had to travel long distances to find food.

Native Americans are the descendants of these early hunters and farmers. By the year 1500, about 30,000 Indians from 20 different nations, or tribes, were living in the Texas area.

Many of the Karankawa made their homes along the marshy Gulf coast and in what later became northern Mexico. On foot or by canoe, these people searched the waters for oysters, clams, and turtles.

When these animals were scarce, the Karankawa ate lizards, spiders, and worms.

In the woods and hills to the north and east of the Gulf coast lived Native American groups that spoke the Caddo languages. These people were skilled potters and hunters. They also planted large fields of corn, beans, and pumpkins. Among the Caddoan-speaking groups were the Tejas, whose name means "friend." The state of Texas takes its name from these Indians.

Mounds like this one were built by early groups of Caddoan-speaking Indians. The mounds were used for burials and other holy rituals.

The Apache and the Kiowa hunted buffalo across the vast Great Plains. These two nations belonged to a larger grouping known as the Plains Indians. Like hunters of other Plains Indian nations, the Apache and the Kiowa followed their prey on foot. While on the hunt, the Indians lived in tepees, which were easy to set up and take down.

Indians in what later became Texas had the land to themselves until the early 1500s. At that time, the king of Spain sent explorers to claim the area that later became Mexico. Traveling northward

Paintings often decorated Kiowa tepees. These pictures are from an ancient Kiowa story about an underwater monster that traps swimmers.

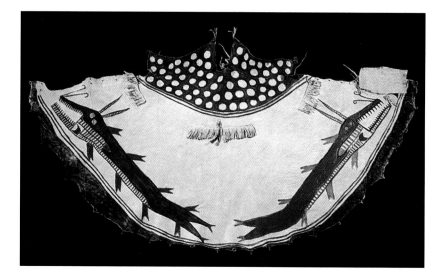

The Rio Grande flows through Boquillas Canyon near the Texas-Mexico border.

from Mexico, the Spaniard Alonso Alvarez de Piñeda reached the Rio Grande in 1519.

Nearly 10 years later, a shipwreck stranded another Spaniard, Alvar Núñez Cabeza de Vaca, along the Gulf coast of Mexico. The Karankawa rescued him and told him legends about riches in cities north of the Rio Grande.

The bell tower at Mission San José is attached to a Roman Catholic chapel. Mission San José is one of five Spanish missions in the city of San Antonio.

In the 1540s, members of an expedition led by Hernando de Soto, another Spaniard, searched western Texas to find these legendary cities. But de Soto found no riches and reported his failure to the king of Spain. The king decided the region wasn't worth exploring anymore.

About 140 years later, however, Spanish priests urged the king of Spain to claim the lands north of the Rio Grande. The priests wanted to set up **missions** to teach the Catholic religion to the area's Indians. In 1682 the Spaniards built a mission near what would become El Paso, in western Texas. In addition to the Catholic religion, the Europeans also brought horses, and the Indians soon began to use the animals. On horseback the Plains Indians could kill more buffalo, which they depended on for food, clothing, and other supplies.

By about 1700, the Spaniards had built dozens of missions, including one among the Tejas. Although the Tejas and some other Indian nations got along with the Europeans, many groups did not. For protection from these Indians, the Spaniards built a

In the morning, Indian residents of Spanish missions went to religious services. The Indians worked on the missions' farms during the rest of the day.

presidio, or fort, near each mission and stationed troops at the forts.

Sometimes farmers from Spain settled near the forts. These settlements eventually grew into towns. San Antonio, founded in 1731 near Mission San Antonio de Valero, was the first permanent European town in the land that the Spaniards began to call "Tejas."

The Spanish priests ran the missions by strict rules. Indian groups herded livestock or farmed to supply the missions with food. In time the Indians grew unhappy with the grueling work and rigid schedules at the missions. They missed the freedom to practice their own religions, to hunt game, and to plant their own foods.

Some Indians ran away from the missions. Many more died from measles and smallpox, diseases that the Indians had caught from the Europeans. Since the Indians had never been exposed to these illnesses, thousands died.

At the same time, a Plains Indian nation called the Comanche had moved onto the plains of what would become northern and central Texas. The Comanche were excellent horse riders and buffalo hunters. They didn't want Europeans to take over their hunting grounds on the Texas plains. To drive away Spanish settlers, the Comanche raided missions, burned farms, and stole horses.

Comanche women hung buffalo meat on drying racks. The animals' skins were then scraped and stretched. Later, the hides could be made into clothes or tepees.

By the late 1700s, Comanche attacks had scared most settlers into leaving. Fearful, Catholic priests deserted the missions. In San Antonio, Spanish soldiers turned one of the missions into a presidio called the Alamo. For many years, few white settlers arrived in Texas, and most Indian groups returned to their traditional way of life.

During a buffalo hunt, Comanche men display their famous horse-riding skills.

Stephen Austin *(seated)* helped hundreds of U.S. farm families settle southeastern Texas in the 1820s.

This situation changed in 1821, after Mexico won its independence from Spain. The new Mexican government claimed the Texas area as Mexican territory. To strengthen this claim and to attract more settlers, the government offered free land to people who would come to the area to live and work.

Many people in the United States were interested in the Mexican offer. Within months Stephen Austin, a U.S. businessman and politician, had arranged for nearly 300 U.S. families to settle in southeastern Texas.

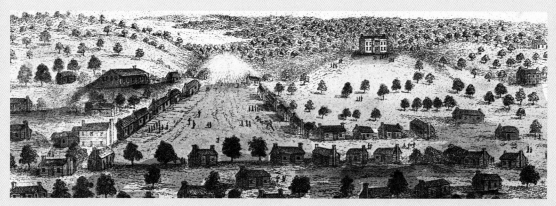

An aerial view of the settlement of Austin in the early 1800s

Both Sides of the Story

In the 1820s, Stephen Austin's offer to give land in Texas to American settlers attracted people who were ready to make a new start. Members of his own family responded, including a widowed cousin named Mary Austin Holley. Stephen set aside a piece of land on Galveston Bay for his cousin.

When Mary reached Texas, she immediately became excited about the settlement. She wrote long letters to her family and friends, describing the landscape and climate of Texas in glowing terms. In one letter, Mary wrote, "The natural riches of this beautiful province have begun to be unfolded to the eyes of admiring adventurers. A new island has been discovered to delight the senses and enrich the pockets."

But a young Kentucky blacksmith, who arrived in Texas at about the same time, had a much different view. Noah Smithwick traveled inland to a settlement near San Antonio. "It was July, and the heat was intense," Smithwick noted in his diary. "The only water was swarming with mosquitoes and full of malaria. Texas looked to me like a heaven for men and dogs, but a hell for women and oxen."

Cotton became an important crop to the new settlers of Texas.

Most of this small group, later known as the Old Three Hundred, were cotton farmers from areas in the southern United States. In addition to bringing farm tools, some of these settlers also brought black slaves, who were forced to labor in the cotton fields without pay.

At first the new white settlers, or **Anglo Americans,** accepted being part of Mexico. By 1835, however, Mexico was under the strict rule of General Antonio López de Santa Anna, who was trying to control the U.S. settlers. He limited their freedom to travel and outlawed slavery. He also would not provide schools with teachers who spoke English.

The growing number of Anglo Americans in Texas disagreed with Santa Anna. They prepared to fight for their independence by forming a small volunteer army. In 1836 about 180 members of this army defended the Alamo against 4,000 of Santa Anna's troops. After several days under siege, the Texas troops ran low on ammunition. By March 5, the Texans could not return Mexican fire. Early the next morning, Santa Anna's troops scaled the walls of the fort, and within two hours, nearly every person inside the Alamo was dead.

The next month, under their leader, Sam Houston, the remaining Texas volunteers won a second battle fought along the banks of the San Jacinto River. The Texans took Santa Anna prisoner and forced him to agree to Texas's independence.

As part of Texas's volunteer army, legendary frontiersman Davy Crockett *(with raised gun)* helped defend the Alamo in 1836.

Mexican general Antonio López de Santa Anna *(center left in white trousers)* surrendered to Sam Houston *(lying down),* who had been wounded during the Battle of San Jacinto.

The Mexican government didn't approve of Texas's independence. But Texans adopted their own **constitution,** or set of laws, and elected Houston president of their country. They designed a flag with only one star on it and proudly flew the Lone Star Flag over public buildings.

The new nation got off to a shaky start. Texas had many farms, but it had few factories and little trade with other countries. Because Texas had so few goods to sell, it was poor. Houston and other Texans realized Texas couldn't afford to be independent, so they asked the U.S. government to make Texas part of the United States.

While the U.S. government talked about this plan, covered wagons rumbled into eastern and central Texas—where farmland was available. The wagons brought settlers, many of whom were **immigrants** from Germany, France, and Poland. Not everyone welcomed the newcomers. The Mexicans, who still viewed Texas as part of Mexico, attacked them. So did the Comanche and the Kiowa.

European immigrants like the Petri family settled in central Texas to farm or raise livestock.

When the United States made Texas the 28th state in 1845, it sparked the Mexican War. The two-year war ended when Mexico agreed to give up its claims to Texas.

It would be 10 years of talking before the U.S. government would allow Texas to join the United States. On December 29, 1845, Texas joined the union as the 28th state. Because Mexico still claimed Texas, this event sparked the Mexican War. After two years of fierce fighting in both Mexico and Texas, U.S. troops defeated the Mexicans. By signing a peace **treaty,** or agreement, in 1848, Mexico gave up its claim to Texas, which became known as the Lone Star State.

Cotton was the new state's chief crop. Most farmers planted and harvested their own cotton fields, but some wealthy landowners had **plantations** (large farms) worked by slaves. Texas was one of many Southern states that allowed slavery, a practice that Northern states had outlawed.

The issue of slavery sharply divided the United States. Northerners were trying to end slavery across the nation. Southerners wanted to keep owning slaves. In 1861 Texans voted to leave the Union. Texas joined other Southern states in a new country called the Confederate States of America, or the Confederacy, where slavery remained legal.

The split between the North and the South led to the Civil War. More than 60,000 Texans joined military units in the Confederate army. Texas also provided guns, clothing, and food for Confederate troops. Cities such as Galveston, Dallas, and Houston grew as new factories were built to make goods for the war.

When the Civil War ended with a Union victory in 1865, slavery ended as well. Many former slaves became **sharecroppers.** They worked on large farms for low wages and received tools and a small share of the crops.

After the Civil War, farmers were attracted by the vast farmland in western Texas and began moving there. The Comanche and the Kiowa tried to drive the newcomers away by attacking wagon trains and by burning farms. To protect the settlers, the U.S. Army raided the camps of Indian tribes.

Quanah Parker: A Man in Two Worlds

During a Comanche raid on a white settlement in eastern Texas, Indian soldiers took a young settler named Cynthia Parker from her home. She adapted to the Native American way of life and eventually married a Comanche leader. Her son Quanah became one of the Comanche nation's most honored commanders.

As a young man, Quanah played down his white heritage by outshining other Comanche in the traditional activities of hunting and raiding. After attacks by the U.S. Army killed his father and captured his mother, Quanah organized more raids. His skill as a commander earned him the respect of Comanche far and wide.

But by 1875, the U.S. Army had forced most of Texas's Indians onto reservations run by white agents. Quanah, one of the last to surrender, was determined to get ahead in the white world but still keep his Indian roots. He became a strong voice for the Comanche, helping them earn money by renting their pastureland to white cattle ranchers. He also served as a judge in an Indian court and convinced white agents of the value of some Comanche traditions.

Within 10 years of arriving on the reservation, Quanah was regarded as his nation's leader. He often represented the Comanche in their dealings with the U.S. government. By the time of his death in 1911, Quanah was honored by many people in both the white and the Indian worlds.

Texas cowboys in the late 1800s drove herds of longhorn cattle northward to Kansas slaughterhouses.

U.S. Army soldiers forced thousands of Indians northward into Oklahoma, where the government had set aside a **reservation** known as Indian Territory. By 1875 the last of the Comanche and the Kiowa had moved to the reservation.

With few Indians remaining in the state, hundreds of ranchers came to the Great Plains of western Texas to raise longhorn cattle. Once the cattle were fully grown, cowboys drove the herds through Texas and Oklahoma to Kansas.

Oil shot 200 feet into the air from the Spindletop Hill well in 1901.

In Kansas the animals were butchered or were shipped east by train. In the 1880s, after railroads were built in Texas, ranchers sent their cattle to Kansas by rail. The railways also carried Texas cotton to textile mills in the northern states to be made into cloth.

Ranchers and farmers grew rich from the sale of cattle and cotton. Some of the state's wealthiest people used their money to search for oil, which they had noticed in water wells throughout Texas. On January 10, 1901, drillers at Spindletop Hill near the Gulf coast struck a vast underground well of oil that gushed for nine days. Before long, thousands of workers were pumping oil from many parts of Texas.

The world's demand for oil increased during World War I (1914–1918). Ships, planes, and other wartime vehicles needed this fuel, and Texas made millions of dollars by selling its oil.

The oil boom started other industries. Some companies made oil-drilling equipment. Others built ships to carry the fuel to worldwide markets.

The Houston Ship Channel, which opened in 1914, allowed Houston's oil companies to send their oil to Galveston on the Gulf of Mexico.

Oil prices fell sharply in the 1930s during the Great Depression, a worldwide economic slump. As the oil industry slowed down, so did other businesses. Many Texans lost their jobs. Some wandered around the state looking for work or even just a decent meal. Others left Texas altogether.

When World War II broke out in 1939, oil was in demand again, and Texas's economy boomed. During the war, military camps throughout the state trained many U.S. troops, pilots, and sailors.

About 750,000 Texans served in the armed forces. Some of these Texans became military heroes. Audie Murphy from Kingston, Texas, won the most medals of any World War II soldier. Chester A. Nimitz of Fredericksburg, Texas, commanded all U.S. naval and marine forces in the Pacific from 1941 to 1945. In 1943 Dwight D. Eisenhower of Denison, Texas, was named head of all U.S. and Allied troops in Europe.

The numbers branded on these longhorns help to identify their true owners, in case the animals wander off or are stolen.

A Lasting Mark

The tradition of branding—marking cattle with a lasting symbol to show who owns the animals—goes back to the beginnings of ranching in Texas. In the mid-1800s, ranchers didn't use fences to pen in cattle. The animals often roamed among herds belonging to neighboring ranches and sometimes wandered long distances in search of food. Branding was the only way to know which cattle belonged to which rancher. The unique markings also made it hard for cattle thieves, called rustlers, to sell stolen animals, because they could be traced back to the true owner.

Ranchers registered, or legally recorded, their brands. Books listed the appearance of the brands so people could quickly figure out who owned each animal. Roundup, the day cowboys gathered and branded newly born calves, was a special event that combined hard work with lots of food and lively music.

In 1953 Eisenhower became the first Texas-born president of the United States. Another Texan, Lyndon B. Johnson, served as vice president to John F. Kennedy. Johnson became president after Kennedy was murdered in Dallas in 1963. Twenty-five years later, voters elected George Herbert Walker Bush as president. He had lived in Texas for many years.

In the late 1980s, the state that had grown rich on oil barely survived a sharp drop in oil prices. Other oil problems arose in 1990, when a serious oil spill polluted Galveston Bay. New industries—such as computer-chip factories and electronics firms—helped Texas's economy keep growing. Although Texas still pumps oil, Texans have found other ways to make a living.

In 2000 George W. Bush, a two-term governor of Texas and son of the former president, was elected president of the United States. As they face the future, Lone Star Staters continue to make their mark on the nation and the world.

George W. Bush and his wife, Laura, in New Hampshire during Bush's 2000 presidential campaign

A bird's-eye view of downtown San Antonio was taken from the Tower of the Americas.

PEOPLE & ECONOMY

A Rich Heritage

hen Texas first became a state, most people made their homes on lone farms and ranches. Many Texans still live in rural areas, but four out of five residents are city dwellers.

Located in southeastern Texas, Houston is the state's largest city. Other big communities include El Paso in the far west, Corpus Christi in the south, and the cluster of Dallas, Fort Worth, and Arlington in north central Texas. Sizable cities in central Texas are San Antonio, Austin (the state capital), and Waco. In the Panhandle, Lubbock and Amarillo are the leading towns.

A traditional part of ranching in Texas is fancy roping.

A father and son wear *charro* suits, the traditional dress of Mexican cowboys.

Texas is home to almost 21 million people, and the number is rising. Only California has more residents. About 52 percent of all Texans have European roots. These people are mainly descended from the German, French, and Polish farmers who settled in the territory in the 1800s.

Another 32 percent of the state's growing population are **Latinos,** whose ancestors came mostly from Mexico. Some Latinos in the state have recently arrived from Mexico, while others can trace their roots to the time when Texas was part of Mexico. The majority of Texas's Latinos speak both Spanish and English.

About 11 percent of all Texans are African American. Native Americans, who once were the only people living in Texas, make up less than 1 percent of the population. In recent years, immigrants from Vietnam, China, the Philippines, and South Korea have come to the state. They account for about 3 percent of Texas's population.

Texans celebrate their many cultures with food, festivals, and music. The German community of New Braunfels, for example, hosts traditional bands and dance groups at its autumn Wurstfest (Sausage Festival). During Fiesta San Antonio, crowds enjoy the city's Latino heritage with spicy Tex-Mex food, bands of strolling guitarists, and flower parades. Blues and gospel music help Texans salute Juneteenth, which honors the day that Texas's slaves were declared free. Texans also enjoy fiddling contests, rodeos, and chili cookoffs.

Traditional Latino music and dance is just one of the ways Texas honors its Latino heritage.

Whether Texans want to study their state's colorful past or explore modern art, they can find just the right museum. The Witte Memorial Museum in San Antonio features exhibits on Indian communities and early Anglo American settlements. At Space Center Houston, visitors can see giant rockets, moon rocks, and movies that were filmed in space.

Visitors to Space Center Houston learn how astronauts move around in a spaceship.

Texas is a sports fan's paradise. The state has a professional team to match almost every taste. The Texas Rangers and the Houston Astros dazzle baseball-loving crowds. The leaps and rebounds of the San Antonio Spurs, the Houston Rockets, and the Dallas Mavericks delight basketball buffs. Hockey fans cheer for the Dallas Stars. For football, Texans can root for the Dallas Cowboys or the Houston Texans. College football also is a big crowd pleaser in Texas.

A marching band entertains fans at a University of Texas Longhorns football game in Austin.

Canoeing down the Rio Grande is a popular outdoor activity in Texas.

Texans who enjoy the outdoors can fish, camp, or hike in 100 state parks and 5 state forests. Big Bend National Park is located in southwestern Texas, where the Rio Grande makes a sharp turn. The park's rugged mountains, steep canyons, and desert scenery show the untouched wilderness of the Basin and Range region.

Austin City Limits, a television show produced in the capital of Texas, features performances by country-music groups.

When Texans are not relaxing, they are on the job. About 64 percent of all working Texans have positions that provide services to people and businesses. Some service workers are bank tellers, store clerks, hospital technicians, and lawyers. Others staff airports, hotels, museums, and restaurants. Some workers load and unload cargo at docks on the state's southern coast.

Government employees make up 14 percent of the Texan workforce. They include city and state officials, law enforcers, and park rangers.

Manufacturing employs about 10 percent of Texas's workforce. Many laborers package food items, including fruits, vegetables, beef, and dairy products.

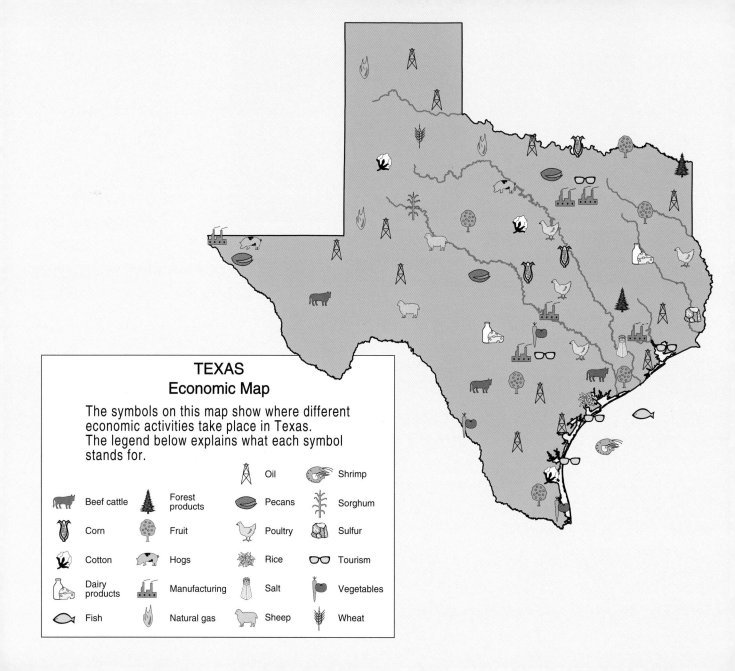

TEXAS
Economic Map

The symbols on this map show where different economic activities take place in Texas. The legend below explains what each symbol stands for.

				Oil	Shrimp
Beef cattle	Forest products	Pecans			Sorghum
Corn	Fruit	Poultry			Sulfur
Cotton	Hogs	Rice			Tourism
Dairy products	Manufacturing	Salt			Vegetables
Fish	Natural gas	Sheep			Wheat

A Corpus Christi shrimper checks his catch.

Factories along the Gulf coast process shrimp, crab, and oysters brought in by fishing crews. Mill workers make paper and plywood from trees cut in the pine, oak, and hickory forests of northeastern Texas.

Workers in Dallas and Fort Worth produce aircraft, clothing, and oil-drilling equipment. Austin is a center for computer-chip manufacturing. Texas leads the nation in making chemicals, plastics, and other products from oil.

Texas's construction industry is thriving. A rise in the number of Texans has created a need for more houses, schools, roads, and businesses. About 6 percent of working Texans have jobs as carpenters, bricklayers, electricians, painters, and plumbers.

About 4 percent of the workforce in Texas is employed on farms or ranches. Texans raise most of the nation's beef cattle, sheep, and goats. The state is a leader in growing cotton and also a major producer of sorghum (a cornlike grass), rice, and wheat.

Farmers in Texas also supply the nation with spinach, onions, potatoes, and melons. Peaches, oranges, and grapefruits ripen in the Rio Grande Valley.

A worker tightens machinery on an oil rig.

The mining industry employs 2 percent of working Texans. Some miners in Texas search for oil and natural gas in underground fields throughout the state. Texas supplies one-fourth of the nation's oil and one-third of its natural gas.

Most people in the state's oil industry live in and around Houston, near the largest oil wells. Refineries near Houston purify the crude oil so it can be used as fuel.

Texas is among the U.S. leaders in producing sulfur and limestone.

A worker checks the hard disk functions on an assembly line of Dell computers. The company is based in Austin, Texas.

Using heavy-duty machines, workers dredge (suck up) sand and gravel from the beds of Texas's rivers and bays. The sand and gravel can be used to make concrete and other building materials. Miners also dig underground for coal, salt, gypsum, and talc.

Some working Texans have stayed with traditional industries, including ranching and oil. Other workers have helped the state expand into new areas of manufacturing, such as aircraft and computers. From rodeos to rockets and from chili to computer chips, Texas is changing with the times, as well as keeping its ties to the past.

Off-shore oil rigs fill Galveston Bay, off Texas's Gulf coast.

THE ENVIRONMENT

Troubled Waters

ocated in southeastern Texas, Galveston Bay is one of the state's most important bodies of water. The bay is responsible for about 40 percent of the state's total commercial fish catch. Every year the bay produces approximately one-third of Texas's shrimp haul and two-thirds of its oyster harvest. The Houston Ship Channel connects Galveston to Houston, where manufactured goods are loaded onto ships that exit through the bay to reach the Gulf of Mexico. In addition, oil refineries and chemical plants line the shores of the bay.

In the bay's protected waters, blue crabs feed on tiny life-forms called algae.

About 5 million Texans live in the Galveston Bay area, which is also an important recreation center. Each year thousands of people come to watch graceful roseate spoonbills, snowy egrets, and great blue herons nest and feed on the marsh grasses at the bay's edge. Fresh seafood makes the bay's restaurants among the state's finest. Beaches lure

Galveston Bay's marsh grasses are the nesting grounds of long-legged roseate spoonbills.

The *Elissa,* which first sailed into Galveston Bay in 1883, was left to rot after years of service. The ship has been rescued and restored. The *Elissa* offers cruises along the Gulf coast, which attracts many visitors to the bay area.

sunbathers, while old ships attract history buffs. Sightseers in the bay area take carriage rides, explore art galleries, and tour historic buildings. People who enjoy the water can go fishing for sea trout and other fish. Windsurfing and sailing in Galveston Bay provide fun for adventurous people.

Galveston residents worked hard to clean up the bay's waters after an oil spill in July 1990.

The buildup of people and industries has harmed Galveston Bay in many ways. Oil tankers have accidentally spilled large amounts of oil into the bay. The oil pollutes the water and sticks to the bay's wildlife, making it hard for the animals to swim, fly, or feed. Cities and factories have dumped poisonous chemicals into the water. These chemicals have killed birds and fish that live in or near the bay.

Machines dredge the bay's sand, gravel, and soil, which are then piled up to extend the shore. A wider shore gives builders more room to create housing with a view of the bay. But marsh grasses are uprooted when workers dredge the bay. When marsh grasses are pulled up, the marshes' birds lose a major food source and nesting ground. These animals either leave the area or starve.

Texans living near the bay have also polluted the water. Some residents pour household chemicals— such as used car oil and paint—down their drains. Through underground pipes, these pollutants eventually end up in the bay.

Human activities have also upset the natural balance of the shoreline ecosystem. Over 70 miles of the bay shoreline have been developed for commercial and industrial use. Continued development of the shoreline contributes to shore erosion, wetlands destruction, increased pollution, and reduced public access to the shore.

A sign warns people that underwater pipelines can leak chemicals into the bay.

This aerial view shows booms. These floating barriers were set up to try to keep the 1990 oil spill from spreading.

Another way people near Galveston Bay pollute the water is by putting too much fertilizer on their gardens and lawns. These chemicals help grass and other plants grow and stay healthy. But rain and water from lawn sprinklers wash off the extra fertilizer, sending it into storm drains. These underground pipes route the water into the bay. Water treatment centers try to filter out the pollutants before they reach the bay, but some chemicals cannot be removed.

In the 1980s, concerned Texans saw signs of trouble in Galveston Bay—polluted water, lower seafood catches, and the loss of marsh grasses. These people met with city and state leaders, as well as with fishing and oil companies, to look for ways to save the bay. All sides agreed that a healthy bay made sense for the state's economy. Fishing would thrive, and birds would attract tourists. Homeowners would have an even more beautiful Gulf view to add to the value of their property.

Chemical plants around Galveston Bay have become more careful about how they get rid of their wastes. Governmental groups make sure that cities and factories dump only the legal amount of waste material into the bay. Companies rush to clean up oil spills with the latest equipment. Next to storm drains, residents have put up signs that read, "Dump no waste, drains to bay."

Children, teenagers, and adult volunteers from the Galveston Bay Foundation are replanting lost marsh grasses. The foundation also educates families about how to protect the bay. Beach cleanups are popular yearly events. Texans hope that these actions will help preserve Galveston Bay for future generations to enjoy.

A mother and daughter bag litter *(above right)* as part of Galveston Bay's annual beach cleanup. To protect newly planted marsh grasses from the action of waves and from animals, workers install fences *(right)*.

Fun Facts

Hot, hotter, hottest! Texas produces more than half of all the jalapeño chili sauce made in the United States.

Thousands of bats make their homes under the bridges in Austin, Texas. At first, people were afraid of the night flyers. But a program to tell folks about the good things bats do—such as eating tons of unwanted bugs every evening—has made Austin a bat lover's paradise.

Texas holds the largest cattle ranch in the continental United States. The King Ranch in southern Texas covers 825,000 acres, an area larger than the state of Rhode Island.

Three of the world's most successful golfers—Ben Hogan, Babe Didrikson Zaharias, and Lee Trevino—were born in Texas.

An assortment of peppers grown in Texas

Texas has more cattle than most states have people! There are about 14 million cattle in the state of Texas.

Dr. Pepper, a popular soft drink, was invented in Waco, Texas, in 1885. It is the oldest major brand of soft drink in the United States. No one is sure how the drink got its name or if there ever was an actual person called Doctor Pepper.

Texas's most-hunted bank robbers were Bonnie Parker and Clyde Barrow. During a two-year period, this Texan-born pair committed a dozen murders and robbed many banks. In 1934 law officials ambushed the duo in Louisiana.

No one is quite sure why Stanley Marsh III, a rich rancher from northern Texas, put 10 Cadillacs nose down in a field near his ranch.

Texas Longhorns

STATE SONG

The official state song of Texas proudly celebrates the state. It was
adopted by the Texas legislature in 1929.

TEXAS, OUR TEXAS

Music by William J. Marsh; words by Gladys Yoakum Wright and William J. Marsh

You can hear "Texas, Our Texas" by visiting this website:
<http://www.50states.com/songs/texas.htm>

A TEXAS RECIPE

Salsa gets its punch from chili peppers.
Almost half of the world's varieties of
chilies are grown in either Texas or Mexico.
Most chilies are both high in vitamins and very
hot. This salsa recipe is simple, healthy, and has
a spicy zing to which any Texan would tip his hat.

TEXAS SALSA

½ onion, diced
1 teaspoon garlic, minced
2 (14.5 ounce) cans stewed tomatoes
juice from ½ lime
3 tablespoons cilantro, chopped
1 teaspoon salt
¼ cup sliced green chilies

1. In a blender, combine onion, garlic, tomatoes, lime juice, cilantro, salt,
   and chilies.
2. On low, blend to desired smoothness.
3. Serve with chips.

Makes about 4 cups.

HISTORICAL TIMELINE

8000 B.C. Ancestors of Native Americans are living in Texas.

A.D. 1500 About 30,000 Indians from 20 different nations live in what later became Texas.

1519 Alonzo Alvarez de Piñeda reaches the Rio Grande.

1529 Alvar Núñez Cabeza de Vaca, who was shipwrecked along the Gulf coast, hears legends about riches in cities north of the Rio Grande.

1682 Spain builds its first mission in Texas, near modern-day El Paso.

1731 San Antonio, the first permanent European town in Texas, is established.

1820s Stephen Austin helps U.S. farm families settle in southeastern Texas.

1821 Mexico wins its independence from Spain and claims Texas.

1836 Mexican troops defeat Texas volunteer soldiers at the Alamo.

1845 Texas becomes the 28th state.

1846–1848 Mexico and the United States fight the Mexican War for control of Texas. Mexico is later defeated and gives up its claim on Texas.

1861 Disagreements over slavery lead Texans to vote to leave the Union.

1875 The last of the Comanche and Kiowa Indians are forced onto a reservation.

1901 Drillers strike oil at Spindletop Hill.

1914 The Houston Ship Channel is completed.

1953 Dwight D. Eisenhower becomes the first Texan to serve as U.S. president.

1963 President John F. Kennedy is assassinated in Dallas.

1990 An oil spill pollutes Galveston Bay.

1993 Republican Kay Bailey Hutchison becomes the first woman to serve as a U.S. senator from Texas.

2000 Texas governor George W. Bush, a Republican, is elected U.S. president.

OUTSTANDING TEXANS

Mary Kay Ash

Mary Kay Ash (born 1915) founded Mary Kay Inc.—a manufacturer and distributor of personal care and beauty products—in 1963. Using innovative selling techniques, Ash has built the largest direct-sales cosmetic empire in the United States, bringing in more than $1.2 billion annually. She is a native of Hot Wells, Texas.

Henry Cisneros

Henry Cisneros (born 1947), from San Antonio, served as mayor of his hometown from 1981 to 1989. Cisneros, the first Latino mayor of a major U.S. city, served as U.S. secretary of housing and urban development from 1993 to 1996. In 1997 he became president of Univision, the dominant Spanish-language television broadcaster in the United States.

Joan Crawford

Joan Crawford (1908–1977) was a Hollywood superstar whose acting career began with silent films. Originally from San Antonio, Crawford won an Academy Award in 1945 for her role in *Mildred Pierce.*

John Howard Griffin (1920–1980), a white writer, underwent medical treatments to darken his skin and then lived in the south. His best-known book, *Black Like Me*, describes his experience with racial discrimination. After the book's publication in 1961, the Dallas native worked to ease communication between whites and African Americans.

Buddy Holly

Buddy Holly (1936–1959), a native of Lubbock, Texas, was a singer, composer, and guitarist whose blend of country and rock and roll influenced many other musicians. Holly's best-known songs include "Peggy Sue" and "That'll Be the Day."

Howard Hughes Jr. (1905–1976), a businessman and native of Houston, made millions of dollars selling oil-drilling equipment in the 1920s. He used some of his wealth to produce and direct movies, such as *Scarface* (1932) and *The Outlaw* (1943).

Lyndon B. Johnson

Lyndon B. Johnson (1908–1973), born in Stonewall, Texas, served as U.S. president from 1963 to 1969. While in office, Johnson pushed through the Civil Rights Act of 1964, which barred discrimination based on race, religion, or gender. His support of American involvement in the Vietnam War was unpopular and eventually led Johnson to retire from politics.

Janis Joplin

Janis Joplin (1943–1970) was a rock and blues singer from Port Arthur, Texas. Her hits include "Ball and Chain" and "Piece of My Heart." The 1979 film *The Rose* is based on her life. Joplin was inducted into the Rock and Roll Hall of Fame in 1995.

Barbara Jordan (1936–1996) was the first African American woman from the south to be elected to the U.S. House of Representatives. Known for her fiery speaking skills, the Houston native was chosen to give the keynote address to the Democratic National Convention in 1976 and 1992.

Barbara Jordan

Steve Martin (born 1945) is an actor, writer, and producer from Waco, Texas. He gained fame in the 1970s for his work on the television show *Saturday Night Live* and later starred in many films, including *Father of the Bride* and *Bowfinger*.

Steve Martin

Larry McMurtry

Sandra Day O'Connor

Shaquille O'Neal

Roy Orbison

Larry McMurtry (born 1936) comes from a long line of cattle ranchers in Wichita Falls, Texas. He used his family history to write the Pulitzer Prize–winning book *Lonesome Dove*, which later became a popular television miniseries. His other works include *Terms of Endearment* and *The Last Picture Show*, both of which were made into award-winning films.

Chester Nimitz (1885–1966), from Fredericksburg, Texas, served as commander in chief of the United States Pacific Fleet during World War II (1939–1945). His strategy of island hopping (capturing only key islands from which attacks of other key islands could be launched) is credited with saving American lives and ensuring Allied victory.

Sandra Day O'Connor (born 1930) was nominated to the Supreme Court of the United States in 1981, making her the first female associate justice in the history of the Court. O'Connor, who received her law degree from Stanford University in 1952, was born in El Paso, Texas.

Shaquille O'Neal (born 1972), center for the Los Angeles Lakers basketball team, went to high school in San Antonio. O'Neal, who stands more than 7 feet tall and weighs about 300 pounds, has also worked in movies and in the music industry. He was named the National Basketball Association's Most Valuable Player for the 1999 season. O'Neal helped the Lakers win the NBA championship in 2000 and 2001.

Roy Orbison (1936–1988) was a pioneer rock-and-roll singer, song-writer, and guitarist. His biggest hit, "Oh, Pretty Woman," sold more than seven million copies. Orbison, a native of Vernon, Texas, was elected to the Rock and Roll Hall of Fame in 1987.

H. Ross Perot (born 1930) became a billionaire after selling Electronic Data Systems, the company that he had founded in 1962. A native of Texarkana, Texas, Perot highlighted his business skills in his unsuccessful campaigns for U.S. president in 1992 and 1996.

H. Ross Perot

Katherine Anne Porter (1890–1980), from Indian Creek, Texas, wrote short stories and novels, including *Ship of Fools,* which was made into a popular film in 1965. Her *Collected Stories* won a Pulitzer Prize in 1966.

Ann W. Richards (born 1933), from Lakeview, Texas, served as the state's governor from 1991 to 1995, becoming only the second woman to hold that post in Texas. Richards's frank, funny speaking style was popular with voters.

Ann W. Richards

Frank Robinson (born 1935), a baseball player and manager, was born in Beaumont, Texas. In 1966 he led the American League in batting average, home runs, and runs batted in. In 1975 he became the first African American to manage a major-league team, the Cleveland Indians. He was elected to the Baseball Hall of Fame in 1982.

Gene Roddenberry (1921–1991) created *Star Trek,* a popular television series of the 1960s. Born in El Paso, Roddenberry was a police officer before becoming a writer. His other television work includes scripts for *Dragnet* and *The Naked City.*

Gene Roddenberry

Nolan Ryan (born 1947) retired in 1993 as one of baseball's greatest pitchers. Born in Refugio, Texas, Ryan signed with the New York Mets in 1966 and played later for the Houston Astros and the Texas Rangers. In addition to striking out more batters (5,714) than any other pitcher, Ryan threw a record seven no-hitters during his 27-year career.

Nolan Ryan

FACTS-AT-A-GLANCE

Nickname: Lone Star State

Song: "Texas, Our Texas"

Motto: Friendship

Flower: bluebonnet

Tree: pecan

Bird: mockingbird

Gemstone: blue topaz

Dish: chili

Insect: monarch butterfly

Shell: lightning whelk

Date and ranking of statehood:
December 29, 1845, the 28th state

Capital: Austin

Area: 261,914 square miles

Rank in area, nationwide: 2nd

Average January temperature: 46° F

Average July temperature: 83° F

After declaring independence from Mexico, Texas began to fly the Lone Star Flag in 1839. The flag is named for the single star on the left side.

POPULATION GROWTH

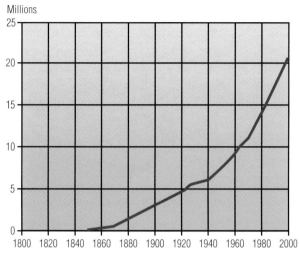

Millions

This chart shows how Texas's population has grown from 1850 to 2000.

In the past, Texas has used many versions of its state seal. In 1992 the state decided to settle on one official version of the seal—a circle of live oak and olive branches around a five-point star.

Population: 20,851,820 (2000 census)

Rank in population, nationwide: 2nd

Major cities and populations: (2000 census) Houston (1,953,631), Dallas (1,188,580), San Antonio (1,144,646), Austin (656,562), El Paso (563,662), Fort Worth (534,694)

U.S. senators: 2

U.S. representatives: 32

Electoral votes: 34

Natural resources: asphalt, coal, forests, iron ore, limestone, magnesium, natural gas, oil, petroleum, salt, sand and gravel, sulfur, uranium

Agricultural products: beef cattle, cotton, grapefruit, hogs, oats, oranges, pecans, potatoes, rice, sheep, sorghum, soybeans, sugarcane, wheat

Fishing industry: black drum, crabs, flounder, oysters, red drum, red snapper, sea trout, shrimp

Manufactured goods: airplanes and other transportation equipment, chemicals, communication systems, computers and computer chips, electrical equipment, machinery, packaged foods

WHERE TEXANS WORK

Services—64 percent (services include jobs in trade; community, social, and personal services; finance, insurance, and real estate; transportation, communication, and utilities)

Government—14 percent

Manufacturing—10 percent

Construction—6 percent

Agriculture—4 percent

Mining—2 percent

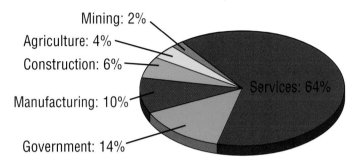

GROSS STATE PRODUCT

Services—59 percent

Manufacturing—16 percent

Government—11 percent

Mining—8 percent

Construction—5 percent

Agriculture—1 percent

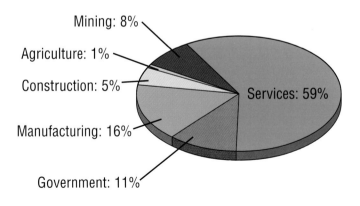

TEXAS WILDLIFE

Mammals: armadillo, bats, bear, coyote, deer, eastern flying squirrel, mountain lion, pronghorn, whale, wild pig

Birds: northern harrier, red-tailed hawk, tundra swan, wild turkey, wood duck

Reptiles and amphibians: alligators, lizards, Mexican burrowing toad, mole, mud turtle, salamander, timber rattlesnake

Fish: bass, catfish, crabs, marlin, menhaden, oysters, red snapper, sailfish, shrimp, sunfish, tarpon

Trees: bald cypress, cat's claw, elm, juniper, magnolia, mesquite, native pecan, oaks, pines, sweet gum, tupelo

Wild plants: bluebonnets, bluestem, buffalo grass, cacti, curly mesquite, daisies, golden rod, grama, primrose, side cuts, sunflowers

Armadillo *(above right)*
Timber rattlesnake *(right)*

PLACES TO VISIT

The Alamo, San Antonio
See the old Spanish mission that was the site of the famous 1836 battle in the Texas Revolution.

East Texas Oil Museum, Kilgore
The museum features a re-creation of a 1930s Texas oil boom-town. It includes an early drilling rig, stores and a street scene, geological exhibits, and a simulated 3,800-foot elevator ride to the oil deposits within the earth.

Fair Park, Dallas
This is the site for the State Fair of Texas. The 277-acre park also includes the Cotton Bowl Stadium, the Science Place, the Dallas Museum of Natural History, the Dallas Horticulture Center, and the Dallas Aquarium.

George Ranch Historical Park, Richmond
Travel through time at this living history ranch. Located inside a 23,000-acre working cattle ranch, the park features tours and exhibits of three eras of Texas history—the 1830s, the 1890s, and the 1930s. Visitors can see demonstrations of ranch activities with blacksmiths, cowboys, and pioneers.

Lyndon B. Johnson Space Center, near Houston
The Johnson Space Center is the training center for all American astronauts. Visitors can tour the facilities or check out Space Center Houston, a special visitors' center. There they can try on space helmets, touch a moon rock, operate computer

simulators, and participate in demonstrations of how astronauts eat and sleep in space.

Museum of Fine Arts, Houston
Visit the oldest complete museum in the Southwest. The museum houses art of world cultures from ancient times to the present.

Padre Island National Seashore, Padre Island
Established by Congress in 1962, this area of dunes and beaches extends about 110 miles along the Texas coast. Beaches for swimming and camping, nature trails, a visitor center, and a picnic area are open to the public.

Panhandle-Plains Historical Museum, Canyon
The largest history museum in Texas features exhibits about the history of petroleum, western heritage, transportation, and art.

San Jacinto Monument, near Channelview
The monument honors the Texans who fought in the battle that won Texas's independence from Mexico. At 570 feet, it's one of the tallest monument towers in the world.

Texas Ranger Hall of Fame and Museum, Waco
Learn more about the famous Texas Rangers, a group of law enforcers that has existed since 1835. The site includes a museum that is a replica of an early Ranger outpost.

Witte Memorial Museum, San Antonio
The museum features history and science exhibits. Highlights include Texas dinosaurs, an Egyptian exhibit and mummy, and historic homes from San Antonio.

ANNUAL EVENTS

Cotton Bowl, Dallas—*January*

Rattlesnake Round-Up, Sweetwater—*March*

Texas Independence Day, statewide—*March*

Cinco de Mayo, Austin—*May*

Old Fiddler's Reunion, Athens—*May*

Texas Folklife Festival, San Antonio—*May or June*

All-Girl Rodeo, Hereford—*August*

State Fair of Texas, Dallas—*September or October*

Texas Rose Festival, Tyler—*October*

Championship Chili Cook-off, Terlingua—*November*

Wurstfest, New Braunfels—*November*

LEARN MORE ABOUT TEXAS

BOOKS

General

Fradin, Dennis Brindell. *Texas*. Chicago: Children's Press, 1996.

Heinrichs, Ann. *Texas*. Danbury, CT: Children's Press, 1999. For older readers.

Special Interest

Branch, Muriel Miller. *Juneteenth: Freedom Day*. New York: Dutton, 1998. Explores the holiday that celebrates the day in 1865 when slaves in Texas learned that they were free.

Bredeson, Carmen. *The Spindletop Gusher*. Brookfield, CT: Millbrook Press, 1996. This history of petroleum in the United States starts with the discovery of oil in Texas in 1901.

Hart, Philip S. *Up in the Air: The Story of Bessie Coleman*. Minneapolis, MN: Carolrhoda Books, Inc., 1996. Learn more about the native Texan who became the first African American woman to fly an airplane. For older readers.

Hoyt-Goldsmith, Diane. *Migrant Worker: A Boy from the Rio Grande Valley*. New York: Holiday House, 1996. This photo-essay describes the life of an eleven-year-old Mexican American migrant worker on the Texas-Mexico border.

Sullivan, George. *Alamo!* New York: Scholastic, Inc., 1997. The text takes readers to the front lines of Texas's famous battle for independence from Mexico. Includes a timeline and reading list.

Vazquez, Sarah. *Cinco de Mayo.* Austin, TX: Raintree Steck-Vaughn, 1999. This Mexican holiday marks the 1862 victory of the Mexican army over the French at the Battle of Puebla. The holiday, which is celebrated in the southwestern United States, is a symbol of Latino unity and patriotism.

Wakeman, Nancy. *Babe Didrikson Zaharias: Driven to Win.* Minneapolis, MN: Lerner Publications Company, 2000. A biography of the Texas-born girl who grew up to be one of the most successful female athletes in the world. For older readers.

Fiction

Gipson, Fred. *Old Yeller.* New York: HarperTrade, 1976. For older readers. In the rough wilderness of the early Texas frontier, young Travis is left in charge of his family's farm. He finds a friend in the big yellow dog that his younger brother adopts.

Jones, Martha Tannery. *The Great Texas Scare: A Story of the Runaway Scrape.* Dallas: Hendrick-Long Publishing Co., 1988. When fighting breaks out in Texas in 1836, two families flee the Mexican army and seek refuge in the open countryside.

WEBSITES

State of Texas Website
<http://www.state.tx.us>
The official site of the Texas state government provides a collection of links to state government agencies, tourism bureaus, and businesses. Also includes links to educational resources and historical and geographical information.

State of Texas—Travel, Tourism, and Recreation
<http://www.state.tx.us/Travel>
Links to sites about nature and the environment, state parks and historic sites, and event calendars offer a wide variety of information about the state.

HoustonChronicle.com
<http://www.chron.com>
One of the nation's ten largest newspapers, the *Houston Chronicle* features local and national news. The site also provides information about the Chronicle In Education program for students and teachers.

JSC Web
<http://www.jsc.nasa.gov>
The Johnson Space Center website features information about NASA and its latest missions. A page for kids provides details about earth and space exploration, games and activities, and expedition images.

PRONUNCIATION GUIDE

Apache (uh-PACH-ee)

Cabeza de Vaca, Alvar Núñez (kah-BAY-thah day BAH-kah, AHL-bahr NOON-yayth)

Caddo (KAD-oh)

Comanche (kuh-MAN-chee)

De Soto, Hernando (dih SOH-toh, ehr-NAHN-doh)

Guadalupe (GWAH-duh-loop)

Karankawa (kuh-RANG-kuh-wah)

Kiowa (KY-uh-wah)

Piñeda, Alonso Alvarez de (pee-NYAY-dah, ah-LOHN-soh AHL-bah-rayth day)

Rio Grande (REE-oh GRAND)

Tejas (TAY-hahs)

A nighttime view of the downtown Dallas skyline

GLOSSARY

Anglo American: historically, an English-speaking white person from the United States who lived in lands under Mexican rule

constitution: the system of basic laws or rules of a government, society, or organization; the document in which these laws or rules are written

immigrant: a person who moves into a foreign country and settles there

Latino: a person living in the United States who either came from or has ancestors from Latin America. Latin America includes Mexico and most of Central and South America.

mission: a place where missionaries work. Missionaries are people sent out by a religious group to spread its beliefs to other people.

plantation: a large estate, usually in a warm climate, where crops are grown by workers who live on the estate

precipitation: rain, snow, and other forms of moisture that fall to earth

presidio: a military post or fort in areas usually under Spanish control

reservation: public land set aside by the government to be used by Native Americans

sharecropper: a person who farms land owned by someone else. As payment, sharecroppers get a house, tools, and a share of the crops they grow.

treaty: an agreement between two or more groups, usually having to do with peace or trade

INDEX

PHOTO ACKNOWLEDGMENTS